KT-430-238

MINDFULNESS
FOR
mums

YVETTE JANE

summersdale

MINDFULNESS FOR MUMS

Copyright © Summersdale Publishers Ltd, 2016

Research by Yvette Jane

Design by Luci Ward

An Hachette UK Company
www.hachette.co.uk

Summersdale Publishers Ltd
Part of Octopus Publishing Group Limited
Carmelite House
50 Victoria Embankment
LONDON
EC4Y 0DZ
UK

www.summersdale.com

Printed and bound in China

ISBN: 978-1-84953-817-6

Substantial discounts on bulk quantities of Summersdale books are available to corporations, professional associations and other organisations. For details contact general enquiries: telephone: +44 (0) 1243 771107 or email: enquiries@summersdale.com.

INTRODUCTION

Being a mum is one of the most joyful and rewarding experiences of all, but it's true to say that a mother's work is never done. The special bond between a mother and child can make even the most challenging task seem worthwhile, but unconditional love can only fuel the body and mind for so long. Slowing down and creating space for calm is an invaluable way to find peace in your everyday life as a mother.

Whether you encounter stress at work or at home, the easy-to-follow tips in this book will help you to free your mind of worries and handle the strains of life with greater ease. There is no quick fix, but these tips will start you on the path to a new, calmer outlook.

When you're confronted
with what seem like
monumental issues,
imagine that you can
successfully handle any
situation. Whether it's
work or dealing with your
child's meltdown, positive
thinking is very powerful
for getting things done.

breathing in,
Calm mind,
breathing out,
Kind heart.

Jack Kornfield

Practise saying no. Reschedule or choose not to do some of the things that, in your deepest heart, you know are not essential to your or your family's life. It could be after-work socialising, extra volunteering or a neighbourly duty. Ask yourself if you and your children would benefit more from a quiet afternoon or evening – necessary for rest and replenishment – rather than trying to squeeze too much into each day. There's no reason to let yourself feel guilty for putting your needs and those of your children first. Don't be railroaded into adding more activity to an already jam-packed life. Your firm boundaries will result in positive reverberations throughout your family.

There is
more to life than
simply increasing
its speed.

Mahatma Gandhi

Place inspiring pictures and notes around your home to remind you and your family to 'be mindful', 'pause' and 'take a breath'. Being mindful is not difficult to do – it's the remembering that's the key! These visual triggers can be all it takes.

Learn to
pace your
energy.

You may settle at bedtime long after your children fall asleep. Appreciate this quiet time and review your day. By letting go of the day's events, you will find it easier to fall into restful sleep.

Add just a few minutes of nothing to your daily schedule, and empty time will begin to work its magic.

Martha Beck

Bedtime stories are the perfect opportunity to set the rest of the world aside and be completely present with your child. Allow yourselves plenty of time as this can be an important way for your child to wind down and get ready for sleep.

Snuggle up so that your child feels safe, warm and happy. Whatever stories are shared – and whether you're listening to your child read aloud or narrating to them – be fully there. Give your undivided attention, knowing that bedtime stories are quickly outgrown and that these magical moments will provide memories for both of you to cherish forever.

The greatest gift you can
give your children is...

your love and your time.

Montague Keen

It doesn't have to be only children who have all the fun. Next time there's a rainbow, join in with the wonder. If it's snowing outside, get your coat on and be part of the enjoyment. Let yourself marvel at nature and see it through childlike eyes.

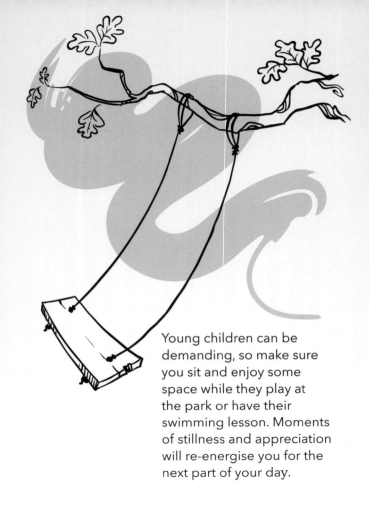

Young children can be demanding, so make sure you sit and enjoy some space while they play at the park or have their swimming lesson. Moments of stillness and appreciation will re-energise you for the next part of your day.

In a family,
if there is one
person who practises
mindfulness, the
entire family will be
more mindful.

Thích Nhất Hạnh

Wherever you are, you
can incorporate a Calm,
Breathing Meditation
into your day.

- Start by becoming aware
  of your breath as it enters
  and leaves your nostrils.

- Breathe to your own
  rhythm.

- Now focus on each breath,
  breathing in the feelings
  you wish to nurture, and
  breathing out the experience
  you wish to create in the
  space around you:

I breathe in calm. I breathe out calm.

I breathe in peace. I breathe out peace.

I breathe in tranquillity. I breathe out tranquillity.

I breathe in strength. I breathe out strength.

I breathe in harmony. I breathe out harmony.

- Create as many lines to your meditation as you wish, with the words that are suitable for you in the situation you find yourself in. It's especially helpful if you're about to do something you feel nervous about: a job interview, a meeting with your child's teacher or any other important task.

There is no way to be
A PERFECT MOTHER,

and a million ways
TO BE A GOOD ONE.

Jill Churchill

Soften your shoulders and take a deep breath.

If you're rushing to appointments and other commitments, give yourself and your children a breather. Stop and encourage everyone to pause and become aware of a few breaths. Then continue, feeling less hassled and more fully present.

DON'T CONFUSE HAVING A CAREER WITH HAVING A LIFE. THEY ARE NOT THE SAME.

Hillary Clinton

It's easy to get caught up in negative thoughts and overlook what is around you and what is really important. One easy way to be more positive in your life is to be thankful. Be thankful for your own body and the things you're capable of. Take a look at your hands that let you do so much, those legs that take you to so many places, those eyes that see it all, your heart and lungs constantly working for your survival. This is a more useful approach than focusing on the body parts you don't like or that are less than perfect in your opinion. Be grateful every day for the good health that both you and your family experience.

Normal day,
let me be aware
of the treasure
you are.

Mary Jean Irion

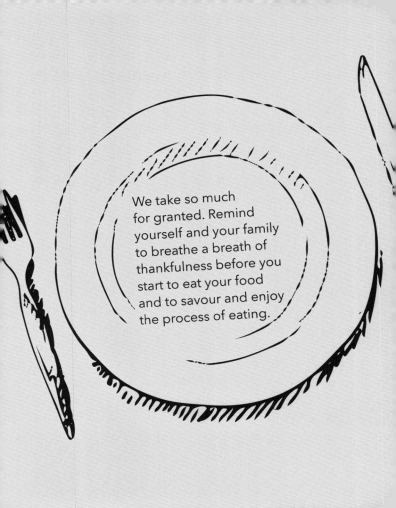

We take so much
for granted. Remind
yourself and your family
to breathe a breath of
thankfulness before you
start to eat your food
and to savour and enjoy
the process of eating.

COUNT YOUR
blessings

TO MULTIPLY YOUR

happiness.

Choose a physical activity
that you love – such as
running, walking, cycling
or dancing – and do it
regularly. This is your
chance to unwind, keep
healthy and reroute
your busy brain away
from stress and overload
for an hour or so.

BE HAPPY.

IT'S ONE WAY OF BEING WISE.

Collette

Our lives as parents are a constant mixture of joys and worries. Difficult events and situations relating to our children can arise in the blink of an eye. Your gut reaction might be to tense up and panic as the maternal instinct kicks in. When this happens, stop and notice where in your body you feel the fear. Breathe deeply into the area, and on the out-breath, visualise the tension falling away. Allow your muscles to relax and your body to soften. Take a few breaths like this to lessen anxiety's grip on you. By remaining calm and anchored, you will help to resolve any turn of events in the best possible way.

YOU CAN'T CALM THE STORM, SO STOP TRYING. WHAT YOU CAN DO IS CALM YOURSELF. THE STORM WILL PASS.

Timber Hawkeye

Carry lavender balm in your bag to massage on to the wrists' pulse points. Its fragrance will refresh and relax you wherever you are, and will calm your child if they have an upsetting fall.

You are
exactly
where
you need
to be.

On waking up, while still lying in your bed, imagine that you are breathing in the morning light. Visualise each breath flooding your skin and bones with golden light from the rising sun. Feel energised as you greet the sun, ready for the day ahead.

WHEREVER YOU GO, NO MATTER WHAT THE WEATHER, ALWAYS BRING YOUR OWN SUNSHINE.

Anthony J. D'Angelo

Travelling to new destinations on family holidays is a great way to view things through fresh, mindful eyes. Soak up your new surroundings – be curious and open to cultures and experiences. Long journeys and unexpected encounters take you away from daily routine and give you the chance to explore the world.

Keep a little pocket journal to note down your discoveries: the sights, sounds and smells. Think twice about rushing on to overpacked sightseeing tours – although convenient, they're not necessarily shortcuts to the best time. Enjoy taking photos but don't look at everything through a screen or a filter. Fully embrace the whole experience and the present moment in order to have a memorable time.

AN AWAKE HEART IS LIKE A
SKY THAT POURS LIGHT.

Hāfez

It's great to hang out with your children but it's equally important to get the balance right by planning some adult time for yourself. Then you can appreciate and enjoy everyone's company without feeling that you – or your children – are missing out.

TODAY I TREASURE MY LIFE.

Housework can feel like a chore, especially when your time is limited. Be completely present as you do what you can – and do it without rushing. Feel a sense of satisfaction at a small job well done instead of stressfully rushing through big tasks.

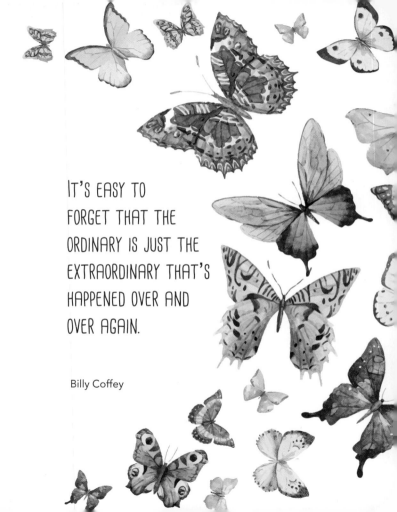

IT'S EASY TO
FORGET THAT THE
ORDINARY IS JUST THE
EXTRAORDINARY THAT'S
HAPPENED OVER AND
OVER AGAIN.

Billy Coffey

The more frequently you multitask or worry, the more your sympathetic nervous system kicks in. It sets off your stress response, sending extra adrenaline and cortisol around your body, causing your blood pressure to rise and your muscles to tense. To reduce this stress response, you can consciously elicit the parasympathetic nervous system, which is your body's ability to return to a state of rest. Meditation is excellent for this – simply sit and focus on some deep, slow breaths. Train your awareness on to each inhalation and each exhalation. Notice the movement of your body as you breathe and be sensitive to your mind throwing up distractions. Continue to refocus on your breath and, within a few minutes, you will feel back in balance, fully alert for your next tasks.

let us not look back
in anger, nor forward
in fear, but around
in awareness.

James Thurber

Stop comparing yourself to
other mums. Every single child
and every single family is unique
and different. Everyone is
juggling the challenges of daily
life and you're doing the best
you can. Give yourself a cheer!

Never give up on yourself.

If unrest is building up around
you, take some deep breaths and
imagine you are growing roots from
your feet into the ground. Stand
firm, while the chaos around you
simply blows through your branches
and disappears on the breeze.

Thousands of things go right for you every day,

beginning the moment you wake up.

Rob Brezsny

Try this Healing Smile Meditation if you are feeling a little low.

Bring to mind someone or something that makes you smile or laugh. Soak in the warm feeling you get when you think about them and curl your mouth up into a smile.

Let this smile gather joy and energy. Breathe it into your heart. Allow the sense of warmth to grow in your heart.

On each out-breath, direct this happy, warm glow around your body.

Let it travel to all your organs, filling them with the healing smile energy. Be thankful for all your organs: your lungs, your heart, liver, kidneys and digestive system. Smile into each of them.

Smile, and let this warm, happy glow travel throughout your body, along your limbs – along your arms, hands, legs and feet.

Keep visualising what makes you feel happy. Breathe it into your heart and keep radiating this happiness out around your body. Enjoy your replenishing, healing smile.

Revisit this Healing Smile Meditation often – it's a gift to yourself!

REMEMBER THAT AT ANY GIVEN MOMENT THERE ARE A THOUSAND THINGS YOU CAN LOVE.

David Levithan

Notice your own inner critic, which may often be negative, and ask yourself if you would speak like this to a good friend. Treat yourself as well as you do others. Kindness and love start within your own heart.

you
are
loved
& supported.

Each time you empty your compost
or visit the recycling bank, thank
the earth for its wonderful bounty
that you and your children benefit
from and enjoy. Encourage and
support your whole family to be
involved in recycling tasks.

EACH MORNING WE ARE
BORN AGAIN.
WHAT WE DO TODAY IS
WHAT MATTERS MOST.

Buddha

Grow some of your own food, whether it's a tomato plant on your patio or a few runner beans and lettuces. Young children love to be involved in vegetable-growing and learn so much from being included in the process. If life is just too busy to grow your own, discuss with your children some of the local produce you buy that is grown close to where you live.

When your family sit down together to share meals, encourage them to ask about the ingredients, be curious about recipes and enjoy helping with the cooking. Use growing, cooking and eating food as opportunities for awareness, enjoyment, gratitude and sharing.

THE KEY TO A

better life

IS BEING AWARE
IN THE LIFE
WE LIVE.

Krishna Pendyala

Even when you're dashing
round the supermarket or
taking the dog for a quick
walk, bring your awareness to
your feet. Slow down slightly,
let your feet firmly connect
you to the ground and gain a
sense of secure balance.

grounded

Being a taxi driver to your children can provide the perfect opportunity to switch off distracting background noise. Turn off the radio, concentrate fully on exactly what is in front of you as you drive and you'll realise that your anxious thoughts have been diverted for now.

LEAVE SOONER, DRIVE SLOWER,

LIVE LONGER.

Anonymous

Give yourself daily helpings of mindful walking!
While crossing from your house to the car, moving
from room to room at home or at work, from shop
to shop, or while walking with your children, there
are numerous opportunities to walk with peace
and serenity. Simply bring your full presence to
the process of walking. Instead of flying out of the
house with a preoccupied mind or with your nose
buried in your mobile phone, be totally present.
Relax your shoulders, be aware of your balance
and how you lift your feet then replace them on
the ground. Notice your breathing and whether
it is shallow and fast. Choose to take some slow,
deep breaths along with adopting a calm yet alert
manner. Your day can be less stressful when you
choose to glide serenely through it all.

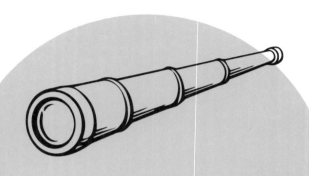

ONE'S DESTINATION IS
NEVER A PLACE, BUT A NEW
WAY OF SEEING THINGS.

Henry Miller

Life can be lively with children around!
Help yourself through the hubbub of
liveliness children bring by

Closing your eyes

and listening mindfully for one minute
today to all the sounds around you.

For one minute,
you have nothing else to do.

Just listen.

Listen!

What can you
hear right now?

Young children are constantly curious and see the world with wondering eyes. They teach us to stop and look again, with amazement, at what is in front of us – a spider, a buttercup or bubbles in the bath. Look anew!

THE UNIVERSE IS FULL OF MAGIC THINGS, PATIENTLY WAITING FOR OUR WITS TO BECOME SHARPER.

Eden Phillpotts

Place your left hand on top of your head and your right hand lightly on your abdomen. Feel into the busy turmoil that you notice in both areas. Now drop your left hand from your head and place it across your heart centre, in the middle of your chest. This symbolises you letting go of your busy mental chatter. Rest in your heart space. Lift your right hand from your abdomen and place it over your left hand.

This symbolises you relinquishing
the anxiety and expectations you
carry in the stomach area. Now
let yourself rest a little longer,
focusing on your heartbeat and
your breath. You can then move on
from a more centred heart space,
having given yourself the chance to
unravel from an overthinking mind
and a tension-knotted stomach.

There is no work–life balance. We have one life.

What's most important is
that you be awake for it.

Janice Marturano

You are probably careful about what your children watch on TV and play on the computer. Also be aware of how violence and negativity in films and documentaries can affect you. Choose what you watch wisely.

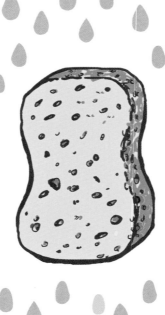

BE AWARE THAT
WE ALL ABSORB
MORE THAN
WE THINK.

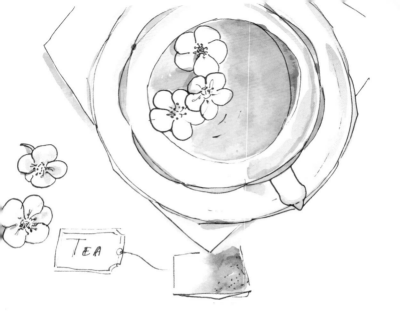

Life is hectic as a busy mum, but whenever you have a cup of tea, ensure that you savour every mouthful. You may be doing other things while you drink it, but each time you reach for a sip, make it a mindful one.

Restore your attention or bring it to a new level by dramatically slowing down whatever you're doing.

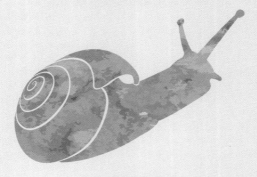

Sharon Salzberg

When you and your children
experience difficult situations,
it doesn't mean you're doing
a bad job as a mum. This is
life in all its guises. Teach
yourself and your family to
start each new day afresh.

I surrender my concerns
by deciding that
harmony comes from
love,

not worry.

Doreen Virtue

WELCOME THE PRESENT MOMENT AS
IF YOU HAD INVITED IT.

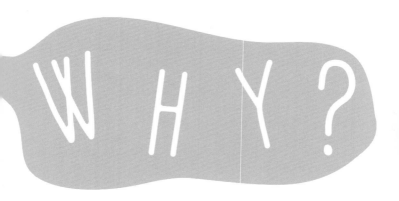

W H Y ?

BECAUSE IT IS ALL WE EVER HAVE.

Pema Chödrön

The key to a clutter-free and calm family home is storage space! Be creative with practical storage solutions and plenty of shelving. Ensure that everything has its place so you know exactly where to find things, thus reducing the drama that arises through lost possessions.

Young children are great teachers of patience. Next time you need to leave the house and your little one is holding you up, smile inwardly because you are being given this learning opportunity. You can either get angry or stay calm – you decide!

Patience and perseverance have a magical effect, before which difficulties disappear, and obstacles vanish.

John Quincy Adams

Encourage yourself and your children to notice the wonders of nature every day. You can become a sharp observer even if time is scarce. First thing in the morning, you might greet the sun and hear birdsong as you pull open the curtains. On your way to school or work, you could appreciate the clouds in the sky or glimpse some colour in the trees. As you work during the day, take a moment to focus on a few breaths while getting some fresh air – in the backyard, on a park bench or through an open window. Remember that nature is a healer and be alert to her constant presence and patient beauty. Always look with fresh eyes, bringing openness and curiosity to your surroundings.

If you have trouble remembering to incorporate mindfulness into your day, place little notes around home and work to act as prompts for you to:

'*breathe*',
'*remember*'
and
'*be mindful*'.

Place a fragrance diffuser near
the entrance to your home or
workplace. As you enter or
leave, you may catch the scent
of rose, wild mint or white
lavender – a great reminder
to stay balanced and at ease.

If you have a pet, give it extra attention and be especially grateful for it today. Your pet is a loved and valued family member and brings joy to all.

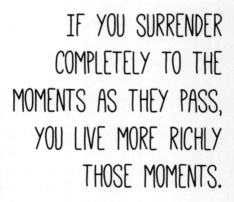

IF YOU SURRENDER
COMPLETELY TO THE
MOMENTS AS THEY PASS,
YOU LIVE MORE RICHLY
THOSE MOMENTS.

Anne Morrow Lindbergh

A Rosebud Meditation is something you can do at times you might wish you were stronger or wiser in order to better deal with life's experiences.

Give yourself some time to sit and meditate. Focus on your breath as it enters and leaves your heart.

Visualise your heart as a rosebud.

Choose a colour for your rose and spend a moment imagining its soft petals and intricate beauty.

Then reflect on the qualities you wish to develop in your everyday life – strength, wisdom or calmness.

Imagine that each rose petal embodies these qualities as it unfurls and opens in your mind's eye.

Breathe in and out, imagining that the fragrance of the rose is filling you with these attributes.

When you feel stronger, wiser or calmer, let the petals of your rose close gently within your heart.

You might like to visualise this rosebud whenever you wish to deepen these qualities.

If you are feeling cross or resentful about your tasks, explore what it feels like to alter your language. Notice what you are saying to yourself. For example, 'I have to pick the children up by 3 p.m. today' or 'I should be working on this project now'. Swap the words 'have to', 'should', 'ought to' and 'must' for 'choose to'. Now you can say: 'I choose to pick the children up by 3 p.m. today' or 'I choose to work on this project now'. Be curious about how this makes you feel. You might notice that these feel like more empowering things to say – let them help you to remember that you really do have a choice and that you really are in charge of your life.

Today I trust myself.

Make today an extra-thankful day.
Notice how grateful you are for your hot
shower, clean clothes, energising food,
fully functioning car, ability to walk/run/
exercise/speak/hear – and, best of all, to
know your children! Blessings in abundance!

Even a small head can be piled high inside with irrelevant distractions.

Etty Hillesum

Sometimes weekend family time can be hectic as you dash about, catching up on visiting relatives and squeezing in shopping, household chores plus children's sporting activities. Plan some leisure time for you and your children to share, like a boat ride, a picnic by the river, an open-air concert or simply a walk together. Switch off mobile phones and other technology and give your undivided attention to being present. Let love and laughter flourish between you as you enjoy these slow-paced, often down-to-earth experiences. See if you can arrange one afternoon a week for these pursuits. Being together as a family in this way provides the best-loved and most vivid memories.

FAMILY IS NOT AN IMPORTANT THING.

it's

everything.

Michael J. Fox

Today I cherish my family.

Keep a journal of happy experiences and grateful thoughts. Our children's early childhoods fly past so quickly – a daily written account, a note of something humorous your children have said or done, can capture the essence of sweet memories for years to come.

On hearing shocking news from around the world, place your hand on your heart and send love and kindness to the people involved. Share this tip with your children so they can develop a sense of compassion through loving thoughts.

WHILE WE TRY TO TEACH OUR CHILDREN
ALL ABOUT LIFE, OUR CHILDREN TEACH US
WHAT LIFE IS ALL ABOUT.

Angela Schwindt

Daily life can feel like a roller coaster. And it's not always the children having the tantrums!

Your body holds on to emotions and experiences, carrying them at a deep, cellular level. One of the key ways to balance your mind–body connection is to stop and give yourself a 'body sweep'. Sit and systematically scan your awareness of your body, down from the top of your head, over your face, the back of your head, your shoulders, arms, hands, torso, hips, legs and feet. As you do this, notice any areas of tension, pressure or discomfort. Allow these to soften and relax a little, breathing into the areas that feel the most tense. The tension you discover might be a 'gut feeling' about a choice you're making or a headache may indicate that you need to pay attention to a health issue. Give yourself the time in your day to do this sweep so you can become more alert to the messages of your body. Be willing to look at your behaviour and emotional state – your openness to exploring these will help you to be wiser in your family relationships.

Not all of us can do great things. But we can do small things with great love.

Mother Teresa

SOMETIMES THE MOST IMPORTANT THING IN A WHOLE DAY IS THE REST WE TAKE BETWEEN TWO DEEP BREATHS.

Etty Hillesum

May I be happy
and peaceful.

If you sense that an argument is about to arise with your child, take a powerful pause and whisper to yourself, 'I can place myself in their shoes, understand them and choose peace in this moment.'

Mindful parenting is a *continual* process **OF DEEPENING AND REFINING** *our awareness* and our ability to be present and **ACT WISELY.**

Jon and Myla Kabat-Zinn

As you move between being a loving mum and a capable, working professional, give yourself a moment to check in with yourself as you transition between roles. On arrival at work, sit still and notice how you are feeling physically – notice any areas of tension that you're carrying with you. Become aware of the mood you're in and the emotions that are hovering around you. Perhaps you're anxious about something relating to your children. However you are feeling, acknowledge how you are feeling. Give yourself time to settle into your work environment, focus on two or three deep breaths, then glide into your workday with a firm resolve and dignified manner.

Flow with whatever may happen and let your mind be free. Stay centred by accepting whatever you are doing.

Chuang Tzu

Spend a few mindful seconds making your bed each morning. Be thankful for your night of replenishing sleep and the place of safety you've enjoyed. Teach your children to do the same, creating a calm transition from bedroom to the outside world.

Pause!

It's what gives you your power.

Care for your hands
with nourishing hand
cream. Be thankful for
all the things your hands
can do, especially as
you raise your children.
Their well-being and
sense of feeling loved
are linked to the gentle
touch of your hands.

There's nothing like

a mama-hug.

Terri Guillemets

Value the power of hugs and cuddles! Hug your children when you say goodbye to them in the morning, welcome them back in the afternoon and say goodnight – don't miss a single one. The human body is designed to produce a feel-good hormone, called oxytocin, when you hug. It floods the body, giving you a feeling of warmth and love. What a great gift for your children to carry with them – whether they're nervous at the start of a new school day, upset on returning home or enjoying the reminder at bedtime that they are loved. Everyone benefits, so don't stint on your hugs!

FOR EVER

NOWS
NOWS
NOWS

— IS COMPOSED OF NOWS.

Emily Dickinson

Spend a
moment resting
your eyes on
something
beautiful, like
a flower, a
candle flame,
a sunset or
your sleeping
child. Allow
your body to
absorb the
feeling of quiet
contentment
and marvel at
the brilliance
of life.

You are complete.

Sing out loud any time and
any place! Nursery rhymes,
advert jingles or pop songs –
the whole family can join in!
Everyone's mood can be lifted
with a giggle and a song.

Happiness...

not in another place
but this place...
not for another hour
but this hour.

Walt Whitman

Forests and woodlands provide ideal spaces for you and your family to go back to nature and to feel refreshed. Soak in this natural feast for the senses. Breathe in the forest smells – the wood's essential oils, moss and soil create magical aromas. Watch beams of light through the leaf canopy and look out for wildlife of all kinds. Appreciate all the shades of green and brown, and enjoy the textures of rough bark and soft undergrowth. There is something for all ages, as you relish your surroundings; young children run back and forth, having make-believe adventures and discovering hiding places; while teenagers may be inspired to sit and write poetry or sketch plants and scenery. Don't forget to take a picnic to complete a memorable trip!

OPEN YOUR HEART.
OPEN YOUR MIND.
OPEN TO LIFE AND ALL
IT HOLDS FOR YOU.

Melody Beattie

There's no end point to being a mum – it's a lifetime role. As you face each new stage, you will learn that the most valuable thing you can do is to be exactly who you are.

Play,
dance.

When you are with others today,
listen more deeply to them and
watch the words you say. Our habits
often go unnoticed and it's easy
to react quickly with thoughtless
speech. Be mindful in your
interactions and see what happens.

Without patience,

magic would be

undiscovered

– in rushing everything,
we would never hear
its whisper inside.

Tamora Pierce

Sometimes you might feel powerless in the face of difficult challenges or people. You know that 'gut feeling' you sometimes get? It's because your stomach area, also known as the solar plexus, is the place where you hold self power and keep your beliefs. It's also the place where you feel fear.

Crank up your power by doing a Golden Sun Meditation.

Gently rest your hand across your abdomen and feel its warmth spreading across this area, like a golden sun.

Imagine that the warmth and shining light of the sun is radiating out and energising your whole body and mind.

Breathe deeply into your abdomen and visualise charging yourself up from the power of the sun, filling yourself with strength and courage.

Create some personalised power mantras to dispel any self-doubt. For example, 'I am calm and strong', 'I create the life I wish to have' or 'I believe and trust in myself that I am strong and courageous'. Use these mantras to connect with your willpower and recharge your inner strength.

How we spend our
days is, of course,
how we spend our lives.

Annie Dillard

I MOVE ABOUT MY DAY WITH PEACE AND CALM.

If you're interested in finding out more about our books, find us on Facebook at **Summersdale Publishers** and follow us on Twitter at @Summersdale.

www.summersdale.com